It just so happens

Poems to Read Aloud

by

Greer Gurland

Finishing Line Press
Georgetown, Kentucky

It just so happens

Poems to Read Aloud

For my parents, Sheila and Ira Hersch

Copyright © 2018 by Greer Gurland
ISBN 978-1-63534-430-1 First Edition
All rights reserved under International and Pan-American Copyright Conventions. No part of this book may be reproduced in any manner whatsoever without written permission from the publisher, except in the case of brief quotations embodied in critical articles and reviews.

ACKNOWLEDGMENTS

Thank you to the loved ones who appear in these poems, for sharing a bit of their own lives, to help me live in a way that is true to who I am.

Thank you to Michael Blumenthal for his friendship, encouragement and enduring faith in me.

Publisher: Leah Maines
Editor: Christen Kincaid
Cover Art: Matthew Hersch
Author Photo: Sussan, Greenwald & Wesler
Cover Design: Elizabeth Maines McCleavy

Printed in the USA on acid-free paper.
Order online: www.finishinglinepress.com
also available on amazon.com
Author inquiries and mail orders:
Finishing Line Press
P. O. Box 1626
Georgetown, Kentucky 40324
U. S. A.

Table of Contents

~1~ Request for Information
Request for Information 1
At the Beach 2
Working Hypothesis 3
[Sad lark] 4
Not in love 5
Trust and Comfort 6
[Yesterday I could not shake this inward feeling—] 7
[It just happens] 8
[I cannot sleep] 9

~2~ Chapter Two
Chapter Two 10
[I inherit this house every day] 13
[You know how people sign orders] 14
[There is a voice in me that says,] 15
Why Am I Pacing the Kitchen Now? 16
Passing Thought 17
I Don't Need You to Save Me 18

~3~ I Can't Tell You How Far We'll Get
I Can't Tell You How Far We'll Get 19
Never 20
You Don't Have to be Superwoman 21
[I learned early not to ask] 22
Little Poem 24

~4~ Bedside Manner
Bedside Manner 25
[I like the simple waves, the ones that keep adrift] 26
Torture 27

~5~ The Test
This is just a test 28
[Fuzzy light evergreens like to pretend it's spring] 29
I am not alone 30
[The beach today is sunshine, sunshine] 31

NOTE FROM THE AUTHOR

I love reading poems because they surprise me. I just found this one in my In-box from the Poetry Foundation's "Poem-a-Day" program. A took a picture of it, so I can hang it on my refrigerator for my kids can see.

Here it is:

> Eros
> By Ralph Waldo Emerson
>
> The sense of the world is short,—
> Long and various the report,—
>   To love and be beloved;
> Men and gods have not outlearned it;
> And, how oft soe'er they've turned it,
>   'Tis not to be improved.

Certain poems like this one are easy for me to understand; they speak my language in a way. I translate: "What we know of this world is actually very little. Both long works on its meaning, and short pronouncements, boil down to the same conclusion: what matters is to love and be loved. Neither men nor gods have found a way to be over learning this lesson, and no matter how many times we experience love, we cannot improve upon it.

What surprised me here is not so much the message—which I feel, and hear, but the simplicity of the way Emerson conveys it. His boiling down of the truth. That is the surprise in this poem. And it rocks me—the way a new song by your favorite artist or a new archeological find might. I will remember this poem all day, and I am fairly certain beyond today. I am so blown away by its power, that it tempts me to stop writing myself; there are no more poems to be written. Emerson did it.

But, at the same time, "Eros" inspires me to keep writing. Any day, any one of us might write a few words that change the day for someone else—and that is an act of love.

And the person who is changed by what I manage to put on paper—maybe I am hoping that will be me, too. Because, the words I write don't come from me. I type away here, but when the words of a poem come, I am just the scribe. It is as if there is an Eros sending me a gift, a surprise. (I am the beloved then.) And it pleases me to find it. Writing it down was simply opening the package.

So I will keep reading short poems—I am impatient and can't wait to unwrap the surprise of thought or feeling which is usually at the end. And I will keep writing poems for the same reason. They feed me. They keep the world new for me. Each surprise changes my perspective—and therefore me—just a little bit. In short, they keep me alive.

~G.G.

REQUEST FOR INFORMATION

Request for Information

We can say it's all good
but it could just as easily all be bad

if we're playing with absolutes.
We're all big and small, lost and confused—

No, that's just me.
The rest of the world is at the beach.

I care little where I am. I am always in me.
How do we wrap our arms around

how big and small we are?
How can we be certain of anything?

I know only what I feel. Everything
else is arguable. O.K., the dishes need

washing, the floor begs
to be scrubbed. Certainly, there is

comfort in what must be done, in spite
of how little we know, and then,

true relief, the most welcome surprise,
comfort when we don't know why:

your words, these walls—
You see them, don't you?

At the Beach

People can tell you about the riptides
but until you've felt one—
that moment of sheer panic—
you don't really know what one is.
I'm not saying you should take your life
in your own hands and wade out deep—
but after all, isn't that what we all do every day,
anyhow? It helps to know what's at stake,
to know what you succeed in steering clear of
on every other day, when you bother
to take just a little care with yourself.
So don't let me off so easy when I
tell you I fell down a flight of stairs.
The fact is, I knew my pajamas were too long
for a long time, and my cartoon fall
was completely in character. It helps
to feel our choices, so we realize we make them.
And we need to; after all, you are
the only one who can save you,
because—let's face it—
you know what you're up to when you did a hole
that's just your size.

Working Hypothesis

Happiness
is having a worry,
and finding out
you didn't need to
worry after all.

Sadness
is finding a worry
you're happy with,
and not needing
happiness,
after all.

Sad lark.
There is nothing in the sky
to be afraid of.
I have seen so much
I don't understand.
The sun rises anyway.
Let's sit and talk about it:
Plates will keep our
knives and forks apart
for generations after me,
and my children will grow to
understand as little as
I do. Comedy will spill
out of the ordinary,
and comfort, comfort,
will mean more and more
to me. It is only sadness that
frightens me. Everything
else that's hurt me
has been a surprise.

Not in love

are the sorry folks
dour in the streets.
Not in love are the teenagers
just learning to weep.
Not in love are the animals
who cannot think, and pine
like I do on solemn nights
when the moon is large and fine.

Not in love are the children
who only know the joy of play,
and sundials that tell time only
in the ordinary way. Not in love
are the keepers of sanity
when there is no finding mine.
Not in love are the wisest men
and women—perhaps
        the one I thought was mine.

Trust and Comfort

Since childhood
I accepted my
separateness
from those around me,
and every suffering
seemed to stay in me.
I would say: "I was not
made for this world."
I said this just to me.
The feeling stays,
my loyal company.
But, today the air is
absolutely perfect:
crisp and still, like new.
The seagull drops his beak
and leaves unscathed his prey,
at least today. I am
of this world. It stirs
in me this
yearning,
bright and sad—
Can I trust you, world,
enough
to let you comfort me?

Yesterday I could not shake this inward feeling—
I did it to myself,
thinking about the past, looking at what I had
written about my own life.
And this morning I needed to write so much,
the words came easily, for hours.
So I look up at grey clouds, now, over
the rocks in the distance, and just want
to sit here in my beach chair.
I'm less afraid of them;
I feel like they're telling me something:
It may just take time.

It just happens
the house is a mess again
and it's my fault. Poetry
doesn't sell, and it doesn't
do floors very well, either.
Nor do I. It's not the poem's
fault that I'm no good at this.
Sorry.
Let's just say I got carried
away by the sound of
words, un-scrubbed,
uncensored; they can wait.
Let's get sponges and soapy
water. This mess is easy
to clean.

I cannot sleep.
Pacing the kitchen at 3 a.m.
I have to ask myself if
a late-night snack
was all I was looking for
when the poem started
talking to me:

"Stop worrying about the noise
the printer makes; everyone
else is asleep. Let's pretend
for just a minute that you
are someone else, entirely.
Let's pretend you've left
the doors unlocked, again,
and that this time someone
entered bearing a message
you will never forget:
The truth is not in
books or the law; it is
in what only you know,
and are sometimes brave
enough to face. Every mark
you buried is poorly hidden.
Go to the shed and get the trowel—
It's not too late:
Unearth for me just one pure sorrow
and I'll write you a great poem."

~ 2 ~

CHAPTER TWO

Chapter Two

In your absence
your teachings echo
just like you said,
in the soft spring wind
I roll the window down
to feel for the first time
since winter's end.
Even a gentle breeze can hurt
if your cheek has waited
for it long enough.

Familiar details do comfort me:
the tethered playground ball
returning to a point,
children on the seesaw, happy
enough to return to where they started;
they are close enough to remember.
It is clear that play is
what they were meant to do.

I wait for the dismissal bell, watching
over my poetry books that obscure the windshield.
On many pages, my Sophie has drawn
in crayon. Why would I stop her?
Art is serious play—and confession.
You said that if a child draws a house
without a door or windows, she may reveal
a secret that helps you to understand her;
Or, maybe the house is telling us:
some doors are secrets even from ourselves—

I think I always knew the day would come
when I would tire of not understanding
this life.

The doors fling open. The children do not need
to be told to run, to drop their colorful backpacks,
get on with real life. What drives them?
The need to move freely? A single child stands still
as if listening to the wind,
unnoticed.
That is a different kind of freedom.

Lately I have tried to count the feelings
I have known. If feelings have shades
like light and color, there must be
an endless number of possibilities—
What is the word for wanting
and not knowing what you want so much?
Maybe I have yet to know how
the answer to my own question feels.
I imagine your suggesting that
a problem so big may have many answers.

Sammy's little bus will be waiting at home
if I don't sacrifice playtime for Russell,
Nathaniel and Sophie. I run
to the blacktop, smiling, dressed
for one season colder than necessary,
waving with one hand, pressing the collar
of my hood to my neck with the other.
(I never understood how to do fashion. Things,
in general, interest me less and less.)
Truthfully, I am still cold.
At least the discomfort tells me that I am
here (I can hear you say this)
which may be as close to "ready"

as I will ever be. Who knows?
You may return and teach me more.
For now, I brace myself for a season
I may never have seen before—
I should be so lucky.

I inherit this house every day
from the me I was yesterday.
Clues as to who I was
everywhere.
I close the drawer, sit
at the table she sat at.
Sometimes I tell myself
she is just in the next room,
baking.
This stills me like coffee.
But I check for cream and
find in the ice box the leftovers
of the pie crust she almost got right.
It is no longer as easy to pretend.
She has gone to visit a dear old friend
I tell myself.
She will be back.

You know how people sign orders
saying what they want done to them
at the end? I just ask that if I'm stuck
in a hospital bed, give me a window
with a tree in it. Not an evergreen,
please, but one with leaves that
change in the wind—even better,
that move in response to how I feel—
why not? How can we ever be sure
what truly moves them anyway? Let
me believe a tree will tell me everything
I need to know. They are persuasive.
This one here hasn't moved all day
despite my staring at it from my awkward,
rumpled bed, imploring it to fall down
now (and I will listen), to drop to the ground
in a heap of brown dust and green
wood, for every good reason or no
reason at all, or just to convince me
that it is the time, now, to end it all.

There is a voice in me that says,
"You're wasting your time.
You're old,
and nothing will come of this
indulgence:
writing and revising,
as if you can change the past."

There's so much to be done:
gifts to be addressed
and wrapped
to thank the children's teachers
properly, a house to clean
and exercises I haven't gotten
back to in days—
all because the words
get hold of me, stumble
inside and take me places
no one should go alone—

So I write them down
to stop them, to appease
the voice in me
that wants the story told,
truthfully—
not quite solid, that voice,
but there, still. It whispers,
as if still afraid
to be heard. But it says,
"What do you fool yourself
that you are saving time for?
You're getting old
Time is running out.
Waste it, waste it…"

Why Am I Pacing the Kitchen Now?

Think.
There is so much I want to do
for me, for you, for the kids—and not
in that order.
No, that is not it.
There is no order to the things
I want to do
for you, the kids and me.
No, not quite.
There is no order to the things I want,
not to mention the kids, me and you.
No.
You, me and the kids *order*
the things I want to do. Hopeful.
But not quite true.
Maybe I am pacing the kitchen now
in the hope that order is not what I
want after all,
but the thinking, and maybe
something about the pace
of wanting; the kitchen floor
is warm and almost smooth, the steps
to wanting
this, just this, and the kids and you…

Passing Thought

You know that moment
when you see a squirrel
in front of the dashboard,
but you keep going,
while you cringe, trusting
that he'll run away in time—
Why can't I believe in
myself that much?

I Don't Need You to Save Me

O.K., I lied. But, don't worry;
If that's too much to ask, I have Plan B:
I will wander the world wearing
a wide-brimmed hat and gather leaves and stones
and seeds, and ask the trees, the ocean and the seas
who made them so strong and so free—
and ask them how to get some of that in me.

And if that doesn't work, I have Plan C:
I'll drive to someplace I have never been—
one where the children look happy and free—
and look into the eyes of the people I meet
and be whomever they seem to see in me.

Or, perhaps a suitable Plan D:
Just to carry on, and treasure
every star, every tree—

I hope never to reach Plan E:
to close my heart-door,
pretend I have not seen what I have seen.

~ 3 ~

I CAN'T TELL YOU HOW FAR WE'LL GET

I Can't Tell You How Far We'll Get

Good. I don't believe anyone who likes making predictions.
I don't mind having a plan; I'm not looking to get lost in the woods.
But every now and then it's a good idea to set out
with just a handful or two of peanuts to mark your way back
and trust in your instincts as a Boy Scout or a Girl Scout
or a human being.

We are still animals that need to hunt for whatever we are
missing in this world. And time is short. Grab a stick and tie
a bandana around the end to hold just what we need for a day
or two. If we survive beyond that, we will have proved
to ourselves we'll have the sense to figure out what comes next.

Never

Every child should know
the joy of a dog licking their face
so hard you have to shut your eyes.
Vito just woke me at 1:24 a.m.
My husband told him "down,"
but I smoothed Vito's fur and said
nothing. The rain is hard, still
we avoided the hurricane. Vito
may not know how far away it is.
Childhood seems near, even though
I am old; does the storm feel
close like that to an old dog,
needing to be useful as ever? Now,
looking in the mirror, my face
is still sticky. Better late than

You Don't Have to be Superwoman

There are no tall buildings here;
anyway, now we have planes.
No one needs to know
how fast you can go.
Think about the energy wasted
trying to be everywhere at once.
Let someone else handle the next thief,
or, better yet, let him get away—
Maybe be will put out the fire
down the street.
Maybe then you can
put up your feet, take off
those painful heels,
for just a moment.

I learned early not to ask
about my namesake, Gertrude.
(Listen to me, whispering her name—
here, alone!) I wouldn't do that to her,
make her cry. But I did wonder
about Gertrude's cause of death,
and if it should worry me for mom.

I listened when mom told us
about the Big Pot that Gerty cooked in,
how it made everything taste good.
"Are you making it in the Big Pot?"
mom said she would ask her mother.
And one day I told my mother, after
having cooked a lot myself,
that I would love to cook in that pot.

But who could find it? It's a recollection,
like how Gerty loved my Grandpa Ruby—
him I knew: plant-grower, story-teller,
Yiddish-speaker who spoke my language
with a thick accent that sounded like a cough.
The thought of my grandfather, now,
at 4:32 in the morning on this earth, stills me.

I imagine it this way from a picture:
Ruben and Gertrude seated at a cloth-
covered table at some family event.
They are the couple who smiles genuinely.
They are open and good, plainly happy,
and generous, like Gertrude's mother,
Molly, who secretly altered her wedding ring
to make a gift of the precious stone
to my father. The "M" in my
middle name is after her. That is how
my mother honored these women
who belong to her: placing the first

letter of each of their names,
a reminder, in me. I will never ask
how much hurt mom felt when she was
carrying me, so soon after Gertrude's death
(and I wonder now if some
of her sorrow could have stayed in me?).

Did it hurt like it must have hurt Ira, my
fatherless husband, to find out I was
carrying a son that his own father would
never see (the only time
my husband cried in front of me)?

***

When mom cooks in certain pots
that look older than me, and she looks up
and does see me, does she also think about
her life that ended right before me,
one I know so little about and yet feel is
part of me, a life that makes mom cry,
too, even though it was perfect
in the memories she's shared with me—

except this story I have heard
so often of when she was small, Sheila
Schwartz, with a birthday each January
twentieth, on which date she would ask
for ice cream, and her mother, Gertrude,
the one she named me for,
would say: *"But it's so cold;*
why not have a Charlotte Russe instead?"

Little Poem

If I could learn to breathe
without thinking
why can't I do more?
"You didn't learn," you say, "you knew."
My point exactly.

~ 4 ~

BEDSIDE MANNER

Bedside Manner

The best physicians
apologize
before they get started;
they know
to heal the wound
you need
gently
to touch it.

I like the simple waves, the ones that keep adrift
the message bottles children send
in second grade to unknown friends.

I like the simple waves—the ones that seem not to care
but carry alike small pieces of bark,
green-black seaweed and tops of bottles broken somewhere. I

like the simple
waves—that seem able to forget
that a tidal wave once set them free, and tonight is restless yet.

Torture

These days of winter feel like spring
And then it's cold again.
Oh, how am I to bear the cold
When warmth's so near at hand?

No one has given reason to me
To accept the double edged sword
Of pain and joy, joy and sorrow,
My lover, my lord.

But there will come a time, I know
When I will wish for now
And feel as wistful as a child
Looking at the snow.

~ 5 ~

THE TEST

This is just a test

If this were a real poem
I would be asking
for complete trust when I
tell you that the waves
that almost meet the shore
crash in on themselves
in mistaken belief
that they've done wrong
by being only who they are,
endlessly; you would be
speaking through the spume
but only to yourself
the words you need most now
to hear, while jewel-toned waves
crashed behind you here: ___.
Beyond them I would wave
to you as you tested
the jeweled cold waters
and listened for a truth that rhymes
with what you already know.
Being as it may, for now,
this is just a test. By all means,
save your strength for
the real thing.

Fuzzy light evergreens like to pretend it's spring
but the forecast is for snow and I refuse
to be surprised at nature's change of heart
again. In fact, I'm taking a break altogether
from reacting to what I think I see. Who am I
to say the evergreen is not right nor
spring eternal? Why does every nameable part
of this world need to signal either life
or its opposite, to me?

I am not alone

on this ship tonight;
the captain steers below.
And when the anchors falls
beneath, the motion tells me so.
But I have no desire at morn
to visit foreign lands.
I only wish to always know
the captain steers toward land.

The beach today is sunshine, sunshine.
Even my grown-up sneakers glitter.
Sammy feels the breeze as he waits
for his turn in the big pool.
No seagulls took my lunch.
A whistle blows. The pool is full
of children testing the limits
of the lifeguard. He has his orders.
I watch a pigeon go after what he needs.
I know he sees me, but he has his life,
too busy to concern himself with me.
Then, a smaller bird—what kind is that?—
hops close then hops away. I am no
danger; he may not know that.
That's OK; I know who I am.

Greer Gurland was born in New York, New York. She studied under Seamus Heaney, Michael Blumenthal and Lucie Brock-Broido at Harvard University alongside classmates Kevin Young and Stephanie Burt. Ms. Gurland served as managing editor of *The Harvard Advocate*. Lucie Brock-Broido selected Ms. Gurland to receive the Academy of American Poets Prize for Harvard College.

After graduating from Harvard Law School, Ms. Gurland practiced law, including special education advocacy. Ms. Gurland is a author of the award-winning book: *How to Advocate Successfully for Your Child: What Every Parent Should Know About Special Education Law.* She has been named one of New Jersey's Best Laywers for Families (New Jersey Magazine 2017 and 2018). She presents frequently to parents through Volunteer Lawyers for Justice and at Children's Specialized Hospital.

It just so happens...Poems to Read Aloud is Ms. Gurland's debut poetry collection. She has returned to writing, which she describes as an indispensable tool for making sense of the world and coping with struggles from the mundane to the existential. Ms. Gurland writes to share "what it feels like to experience the truths that we all do, but from my eyes." She aims to write poetry that is easy to read and to understand but that captures the complexities that defy understanding. Her work is informed by her own experiences—which include finding her way back to writing after years looking to discover her own answer to how to forge meaning in the small moments and the large ones that shape our lives.

Ms. Gurland's poetry and creative non-fiction have appeared in publications including *The Harvard Advocate*, *The Harvard Quarterly* and *Sweet* literary magazine. In 2017, she was awarded a fellowship from the Martha's Vineyard Creative Writing Institute. Ms. Gurland is the current recipient of The Mitch and Lynn Baumeister Scholarhip in Creative Writing at Fairleigh Dickinson University where she is a candidate in their MFA in Poetry Program, studying under Harvey L. Hix and Jeffrey Allen.

Ms. Gurland and her husband live in Westfield, New Jersey with their five young children.

www.ingramcontent.com/pod-product-compliance
Lightning Source LLC
LaVergne TN
LVHW041601070426
835507LV00011B/1243